Experiences in Social Psychology
Active Learning Adventures

Gary G. Brannigan
State University of New York, Plattsburgh

Allyn and Bacon
Boston London Toronto Sydney Tokyo Singapore

Copyright © 2002 by Allyn & Bacon
A Pearson Education Company
75 Arlington Street
Boston, Massachusetts 02116

Internet: www.ablongman.com

ISBN 0-205-33652-3

Printed in the United States of America

10 9 8 7 6 5 4 3 2 1   04 03 02 01

Contents

ABOUT THE AUTHOR

Gary G. Brannigan (Ph.D., University of Delaware) is a Professor of Psychology at SUNY-Plattsburgh, where he has taught for nearly 30 years. He also served as Director of the Psychological Services Clinic at SUNY-Plattsburgh and was a consultant to several local agencies. His research focuses primarily on psychological assessment and therapy with children. He was elected to the status of Fellow in the Society for Personality Assessment, and has served on the editorial boards of four journals. In addition to coediting *The Undaunted Psychologist: Adventures in Research, The Social Psychologists: Research Adventures, The Developmental Psychologists: Research Adventures Across the Life Span*, and *The Sex Scientists*, and editing *The Enlightened Educator: Research Adventures in the Schools*, and *The Sport Scientists: Research Adventures*, he has published numerous articles, chapters, books, and tests, including *Research and Clinical Applications of the Bender-Gestalt Test, Experiences in Personality: Research, Assessment, and Change, Experiencing Psychology: Active Learning Adventures*, and *The Modified Version of the Bender-Gestalt Test* (now in its second edition).

PREFACE

Experiences in Social Psychology: Active Learning Adventures contains thirty-two active learning experiences that correspond to major topics covered in social psychology:

research design	the self
social beliefs and judgments	attitudes
conformity	stereotyping
group behavior	discrimination
prejudice	aggression
altruism	interpersonal attraction
relationships	health
legal issues	conflict

The book was designed to aid instructors in providing quality experiences for students. Each student will have access to all the material needed to complete activities. So, there is no need for instructors to obtain permissions to use copyrighted items, make copies of materials, or utilize precious class time to conduct activities. Rather, students will come to class armed with first-hand experiences in the subject matter.

The activities can be used to supplement instruction and enhance learning by providing students with opportunities to explore theories and concepts in social psychology. Although they are designed as out-of-classroom assignments, the activities are rich with possibilities for in-class use. For example, you can collate students' responses, develop class norms, and compare, contrast, and discuss responses in large or small group formats. Students generally enjoy this approach because they are not merely passive recipients of knowledge.

You should feel free to adjust activities to suit the needs of your course (e.g., adding, deleting, or modifying questions). In fact, I would appreciate your suggestions for improving any of the activities. I can be reached at the Department of Psychology, State University of New York–Plattsburgh, Plattsburgh, New York 12901 (e-mail: Gary.Brannigan@plattsburgh.edu).

Acknowledgments

I deeply appreciate the assistance of Carolyn Merrill. Her counsel and support enhanced the quality of this book. Four anonymous reviewers also provided valuable suggestions for clarifying and improving activities. I greatly appreciate their efforts.

I am grateful to the State University of New York - Plattsburgh for providing the supportive environment that enabled me to pursue this project. The advice of my colleagues, especially Bill Tooke and Renee Bator, was invaluable. I also wish to thank the many students who helped to field test these activities. Their suggestions made this book more student-focused and accessible.

My long time friend and secretary, Judy Dashnaw, edited, formatted, and word processed this book. Her meticulous attention to details and dedication to this work immensely improved the final product.

Finally, I wish to thank my wife, Linda, for her inspiration and ongoing support.

INTRODUCTION

Experiences in Social Psychology: Active Learning Adventures is designed to be used as a supplement to traditional social psychology texts. Although textbooks do an excellent job of transmitting basic information, they do not give readers a true feel for what actually is being done to collect that information. Over the past 10 years, I have been working to provide readers with materials that give them a clearer sense of what psychology is all about.

My first attempt to achieve the goal of involving students in psychology resulted in several books (see References) that revolved around first-person accounts of how and why scientists do what they do. Although the stories provided interesting details about the personal and professional factors that influence scientists' work, as well as in-depth coverage of major research projects, I noted that they were no substitute for first-hand experience.

This is my second attempt to reach this goal (and my third book of this type—see References). The activities are designed to involve you in the excitement of discovery and allow you to personally explore the theories and concepts you encounter in social psychology. You will not only think about but actually participate in the topics you study. This will make the process of learning more dynamic and meaningful and will give you a clearer understanding of yourself and the world around you.

Throughout the book, you will be collecting data on yourself and others. When you use other people as subjects, you or your instructor will likely need to receive permission from a special campus committee established to protect human subjects. When you complete an experiment, be sure to adhere strictly to their guidelines; thoroughly "debrief" your subject about the nature of the experiment and answer all of his or her questions.

Finally, in addition to being interesting, informative, and challenging, the activities should be fun. I hope you enjoy your adventures.

References

Brannigan, G. G. (Ed.) (1996). *The enlightened educator: Research adventures in the schools*. New York: McGraw-Hill.

Brannigan, G. G. (Ed.) (1999). *The sport scientists: Research adventures*. New York: Longman.

Brannigan, G. G. (2000). *Experiencing psychology: Active learning adventures*. Upper Saddle River, NJ: Prentice-Hall.

Brannigan, G. G., Allgeier, E. R., & Allgeier, A. R. (Eds.) (1998). *The sex scientists*. New York: Longman.

Brannigan, G. G., & Merrens, M. R. (Eds.) (1993). *The undaunted psychologist: Adventures in research*. New York: McGraw-Hill.

Brannigan, G. G., & Merrens, M. R. (Eds.) (1995). *The social psychologists: Research adventures.* New York: McGraw-Hill.

Merrens, M. R., & Brannigan, G. G. (Eds.) (1996). *The developmental psychologists: Research adventures across the life span.* New York: McGraw-Hill.

Merrens, M. R., & Brannigan, G. G. (1998). *Experiences in personality: Research, assessment, and change.* New York: Wiley.

CHAPTER 1

Introduction to Social Psychology

Name _____

Active Learning Experience

1.1 Impressions

Before reading further, rate your instructor on the following 20 item scale, adapted from Robert McCrae and Paul Costa's (1987) five factor model of personality.

Instructor Rating

Rate your instructor on the following dimensions by circling the appropriate number on the five-point scale.

1. Down to Earth   Imaginative
    1   2   3   4   5

2. Lazy   Hard Working
    1   2   3   4   5

3. Secure   Insecure
    1   2   3   4   5

4. Reserved   Affectionate
    1   2   3   4   5

5. Callous   Sympathetic
    1   2   3   4   5

6. Comfortable   Self-conscious
    1   2   3   4   5

7. Uncooperative   Helpful
    1   2   3   4   5

8. Narrow Interests   Broad Interests
    1   2   3   4   5

9. Quiet   Talkative
    1   2   3   4   5

10. Negligent — Conscientious

1	2	3	4	5

11. Calm — Worrying

1	2	3	4	5

12. Aloof — Friendly

1	2	3	4	5

13. Conventional — Original

1	2	3	4	5

14. Aimless — Ambitious

1	2	3	4	5

15. Vengeful — Forgiving

1	2	3	4	5

16. Even-tempered — Temperamental

1	2	3	4	5

17. Retiring — Sociable

1	2	3	4	5

18. Quitting — Persevering

1	2	3	4	5

19. Unadventurous — Daring

1	2	3	4	5

20. Irritable — Good-natured

1	2	3	4	5

Scoring: Total the scores for each of the five dimensions and divide each by 4.

Openness to Experience (0) :	1, 8, 13, and 19
Conscientiousness (C) :	2, 10, 14, and 18
Extraversion (E) :	4, 9, 12, and 17
Agreeableness (A):	5, 7, 15, and 20
Neuroticism (N) :	3, 6, 11, and 16

Ratings

O   _____

C   _____

E   _____

A   _____

N   _____

These five dimensions are thought by many to be "basic" descriptions of personality. In interpreting the scores, you can get an idea of where you think your instructor falls on each dimension by how far your score is from the midpoint (3) of the scale. The higher the score, the higher your instructor is on that dimension.

Also answer the following questions (adapted from Lashley, 1987) about your instructor, based on your impressions.

1.   Age _____

2.   Marital status _____

3.   Favorite type of music _____

4.   Favorite color _____

5.   Favorite type of TV show _____

6.   Favorite leisure activity _____

7.   From what country (if USA, what region? state?) _____

_____

6

8. Favorite sport (spectator) _____

    (participant) _____

9. Favorite type of book: _____

This activity should serve as an introduction to social psychology. As you review your responses with your instructor, you should gain an understanding of your implicit theories about people, specifically, traits that characterize people of a particular age, gender, and occupation.

In the absence of other information, we use these theories to form impressions of others. As Robin Lashley (1987) noted, "students expect the typical teacher to be a married, conservative, introverted intellectual who prefers dark colors, sedentary hobbies, and structured vacations." (p. 180). On the five factors of personality, I have found that students rate the concept "Professor" as only mildly Open to Experience and Extraverted, high in Conscientiousness and Agreeableness, and low in Neuroticism.

How did your responses compare with these findings?

Based on this experience, what did you learn about your implicit theories of people?

References

Lashley, R. L. (1987). Using students' perceptions of their instructor to illustrate principles of person perceptions. *Teaching of Psychology, 14*, 179-180.

McCrae, R., & Costa, P. (1987). Validation of the five-factor model of personality across instruments and observers. *Journal of Personality and Social Psychology, 52*, 81-90.

8

Name _____

Active Learning Experience

1.2 Experimental Design

Given the human resources in your classroom, design an experiment to test this belief: **Women are particularly susceptible to flattery and thus tend to comply with requests when given compliments.**

1. What is your hypothesis?

2. How would you select your subjects?

3. What is your independent variable? Give a detailed description of the experimental procedure you would follow.

4. What is your dependent variable?

5. Are there any limitations in interpreting the potential results of the experimental test of your hypothesis? If so, describe them.

12

Snyder and Gangestad (1981) used this task to test another assumption: When individuals collect information to test stereotypes, they spend more time and energy collecting evidence to confirm than to disconfirm the stereotypes. On this task, they reported that only about one-third of their research participants adequately designed their research to fairly test the hypothesis under question! If you fell prey to this "confirmatory bias," how can you redesign your experiment to account for this bias? Hint: Most people include the condition where "females are flattered," but other conditions are needed!

Reference

Snyder, M., & Gangestad, S. (1981). Hypothesis-testing process. In J. H. Harvey, W. Ickes, & R. F. Kidd (Eds.), *New directions in attribution research, (Vol. 3)* (pp. 171-196). Hillsdale, NJ: Erlbaum.

CHAPTER 2

The Self

14

Name _____

Active Learning Experience

2.1 Who Are You?

Before reading further, write twenty answers to the question "Who am I?" in the spaces below.

1. _____

2. _____

3. _____

4. _____

5. _____

6. _____

7. _____

8. _____

9. _____

10. _____

11. _____

12. _____

13. _____

14. _____

15. _____

16. _____

17. _____

18. _____

19. _____

20. _____

This procedure was developed by Manford Kuhn and Thomas McPartland (1954) to identify and measure self-attitudes. They believed that human behavior is organized and directed by the individual's attitudes toward himself or herself.

Your responses are what you consider central to who you are! This is not a static process, but one that has changed over time and will continue to change in the future. Raymond Montemayor and Marvin Eisen (1977) noted "a developmental increase in the depth and vividness of self-conceptions. Children describe where they live, what they look like, and what they do. Their self-concept seems. . .undifferentiated, both from other people and from their environment. Adolescents, however, describe themselves in terms of their beliefs and personality characteristics, qualities which are more essential and intrinsic to the self and which produce a picture of the self that is sharp and unique." (p. 318)

In addition to age differences, how would gender and/or cultural (e.g., individualistic vs collectivistic) factors affect people's responses on this task? Explain.

Describe the impact of age, gender, and culture on who you are.

How "central" do you think your responses on this task are to who you are?

Joan Rentsch and Tonia Heffner (1997) added another element to this procedure that you may want to try. "Rank order each answer in terms of how important it is to the way you generally feel about yourself" (p. 644), with 1 indicating the most important component. Then, "rate whether or not you are satisfied with each answer as it represents a particular aspect of yourself" (p. 644), on a six-point scale (1 = very dissatisfied to 6 = very satisfied).

Once you complete these ratings, you can examine your satisfaction with your self-concept. How satisfied are you with items most central to who you are?

If there are items that are central to your self-concept that you are not satisfied with, why is this the case? What can you do to change this situation?

References

Kuhn, M. H., & McPartland (1954). An empirical investigation of self-attitudes. *American Sociological Review, 19*, 68-76.

Montemayor, R., & Eisen, M. (1977). The development of self-conceptions from childhood to adolescence. *Developmental Psychology, 13*, 314-319.

Rentsch, J. R., & Heffner, T. S. (1992). Measuring self-esteem: Validation of a new scoring technique for "Who Am I?" responses. *Educational and Psychological Measurement, 52*, 641-651.

20

Active Learning Experience

2.2 Strengths and Weaknesses

This activity should be done anonymously. Do not include any identifying information.

Before reading further, make a list of what you consider your personal "strengths" and "weaknesses" in the space below.

Strengths | Weaknesses

How many strengths did you list? _____

How many weaknesses did you list? _____

    If you listed more personal strengths than weaknesses, you are not alone. Dana Dunn (1989) designed and conducted this activity in various social psychology classes. Students generally reported about twice as many strengths as weaknesses!

    Anthony Greenwald (1995) linked this behavior to a bias called "beneffectance," which is part of an elaborate system designed to protect the "self." "In judging the self... we see ourselves as having more than our fair share of good qualities and also more than others are inclined to credit us with" (p. 6). He went on to state that this "system" impacts many aspects of our lives. Most notably, "in observing others, we most easily notice characteristics that are central to our own personalities. . . . We readily believe that successes fairly reflect our abilities. . . . We avoid taking responsibility for failure. . . . And we smoothly reconstruct memories of our past to make [them]. . .consistent with our present self-image" (p. 6).

    How does the knowledge of this self-serving bias affect your view of your "self"? Explain.

How would cultural (e.g., individualistic vs collectivistic) factors affect the self-serving bias?

References

Dunn, D. (1989). Demonstrating a self-serving bias. *Teaching of Psychology, 16*, 21-22.

Greenwald, A. G. (1995). Getting (my) self into social psychology. In G. G. Brannigan & M. R. Merrens (Eds.). *The social psychologists: Research adventures* (pp. 2-16) New York: McGraw-Hill.

Name _____

Active Learning Experience

2.3 Interactions

List your favorite activity and the same-sex person you most like to engage in that activity with for each of the following five leisure activities.

Leisure Pursuits

1. Non-competitive recreational activities.
    Your favorite activity: _____
    Who is the same-sex person you most like to engage in this activity with? _____
    _____
    Why did you choose this person? _____
    _____

2. Competitive recreational activities.
    Your favorite activity: _____
    Who is the same-sex person you most like to engage in this activity with? _____
    _____
    Why did you choose this person? _____
    _____

3. Party-going activities.
    Your favorite activity: _____
    Who is the same-sex person you most like to engage in this activity with? _____
    _____
    Why did you choose this person? _____
    _____

4. Live entertainment activities.
    Your favorite activity: _____
    Who is the same-sex person you most like to engage in this activity with? _____
    _____
    Why did you choose this person? _____
    _____

5. Cultural activities.
    Your favorite activity: _____
    Who is the same-sex person you most like to engage in this activity with? _____
    _____
    Why did you choose this person? _____
    _____

Dating

6. Are you currently dating someone exclusively (one person and no one else)?
   Yes _____   No _____

7. If yes, how many months have you dated this person?

   _____

8. How many different persons have you dated in this past year?

   _____

Complete the following questionnaire. The statements below concern your personal reactions to a number of different situations. No two statements are exactly alike, so consider each statement carefully before answering. If a statement is TRUE or MOSTLY TRUE as applied to you, circle the "T." If a statement is FALSE or NOT USUALLY TRUE as applied to you, circle the "F."

T   F   1. I find it hard to imitate the behavior of other people.

T   F   2. At parties and social gatherings, I do not attempt to do or say things that others will like.

T   F   3. I can only argue for ideas which I already believe.

T   F   4. I can make impromptu speeches even on topics about which I have almost no information.

T   F   5. I guess I put on a show to impress or entertain people.

T   F   6. I would probably make a good actor.

T   F   7. In a group of people I am rarely the center of attention.

T   f   8. In different situations and with different people, I often act like very different persons.

T   F   9. I am not particularly good at making other people like me.

T   F   10. I'm not always the person I appear to be.

T   F   11. I would not change my opinions (or the way I do things) in order to please someone else or win their favor.

T   F   12. I have considered being an entertainer.

T   F   13. I have never been good at games like charades or improvisational acting.

T   F   14. I have trouble changing my behavior to suit different people and different situations.

T   F   15. At a party I let others keep the jokes and stories going.

T   F   16. I feel a bit awkward in company and do not show up quite so well as I should.

T   F   17. I can look anyone in the eye and tell a lie with a straight face (if for a right end).

T   F   18. I may deceive people by being friendly when I really dislike them.

28

Scoring

To score the scale, give one point for each of the following questions answered "True": 4, 5, 6, 8, 10, 12, 17, and 18, and one point for each of the following questions answered "False": 1, 2, 3, 7, 9, 11, 13, 14, 15, and 16. Total the score. High scores indicate higher self-monitoring.

Score =

In class, determine the median score for the total class:

Median =

Those scoring above the median are *high* self-monitors. Those scoring below the median are *low* self-monitors.

Mark Snyder (1995) differentiated between high and low self-monitors in the following way. High self-monitors possess "a repertoire of different selves from which they can choose the one that best fits their current surroundings. . . .Low self-monitors. . . value congruence between who they are and what they do (p. 37).

Snyder and his colleagues (1983, 1984, 1986, 1988) designed and conducted the experiments that form the basis for this activity. Generally, they found that high self-monitors were more likely than low self-monitors to choose different people to engage in different activities. They are also less likely to be exclusive daters and are more likely to have dated a greater number of people.

How did your results and the results of your classmates compare with Snyder's findings?

leisure pursuits -

dating -

What other aspects of your life are affected by your self-monitoring style? Explain.

What are the assets and liabilities of your style?

References

Simpson, J. A. (1988). Self-monitoring and commitment to dating relationships: A classroom demonstration. *Teaching of Psychology, 5,* 1-33.

Snyder, M. (1995). Self-monitoring: Public appearances versus private realities. In G. G. Brannigan & Mr. R. Merrens (Eds.), *The social psychologist: Research adventures* (pp. 34-50). New York: McGraw-Hill.

Snyder, M., Gangestad, S., & Simpson, J. A. (1983). Choosing friends as activity partners: The role of self-monitoring. *Journal of Personality and Social Psychology, 45,* 1061-1072.

Snyder, M., & Gangestad, S. (1986). On the nature of self-monitoring: Matters of assessment, matters of validity. *Journal of Personality and Social Psychology, 51* (1), 125-139.

Snyder, M., & Simpson, J. A. (1984). Self-monitoring and dating relationships. *Journal of Personality and Social Psychology, 47,* 1281-1291.

CHAPTER 3

Social Beliefs and Judgments

Name _____

Active Learning Experience

3.1 Schemas and Sets

Before reading further, follow the directions below.

Read the following story. Then, describe the specific activity that is being discussed.

> The procedure is actually quite simple. First you arrange items into different groups. Of course one pile may be sufficient depending on how much there is to do. If you have to go somewhere else due to lack of facilities that is the next step; otherwise, you are pretty well set. It is important not to overdo things. That is, it is better to do too few things at once than too many. In the short run this may not seem important but complications can easily arise. A mistake can be expensive as well. At first, the whole procedure will seem complicated. Soon, however, it will become just another facet of life. It is difficult to foresee any end to the necessity for this task in the immediate future, but then, one can never tell. After the procedure is complete, one arranges the materials into their appropriate places. Eventually, they will be used once more and the whole cycle will then have to be repeated. However, this is part of life (p. 722). From Bransford, J. D., & Johnson, M. K. (1972). Contextual prerequisites for understanding: Some investigations of comprehension and recall. *Journal of Verbal Learning and Verbal Behavior, 11,* 717-726. Copyright © 1972 by Academic Press. Reprinted with permission.

What thoughts do you have about what is going on in this story?

Turn the page only after you have exhausted your thoughts.

If you had difficulty trying to figure out what specific activity was being discussed in the story, you are not alone. Many people find it difficult to attach meaning to the events related. This difficulty arises, in part, because it is difficult to find an effective schema for these events. Schemas help us to make sense of our world by organizing our knowledge around themes.

Can you imagine what it would be like to go through life without the ability to use schemas--to have every situation and encounter seem like the one you just read?

You may still be thinking about possible schemas to link what seems to be disparate events in this story. Here are some for you to consider. Reread the story. But, this time, try the following schemas one at a time and see how they work.

Describe your thoughts as you try each schema.

Sorting playing cards -

Baking cookies -

Doing the laundry -

Delivering the mail -

What do you conclude from this experience?

Expectations or sets also play important roles in our day-to-day lives. They allow us to prepare for situations in advance and to make decisions.

Below is an example of a task that demonstrates the role of mental sets in problem solving.

At one time or another, you have likely encountered problems that ask you to predict the next number in a sequence. Write down your thoughts about possible solutions as you try to solve this problem. When you solve the problem or exhaust all your solutions, turn to the next page.

What is the next number in this sequence?

    8   5   9   1   7   2   _____

Thoughts:

If your attempts to solve this problem were numerically based, then you have fallen into a common trap. Mental sets, or tendencies to approach problems in certain ways based on our previous experiences, may work against us in problem-solving situations. Your mental set was that the numbers were in some logical *numerical* sequence.

As you struggled with the problem, did any other possible sequence--like a language-based one--cross your mind? Try again, this time exploring language-based solutions. Write down your thoughts as you explore solutions. When you solve the problem or exhaust all your solutions, turn to the next page.

Eight   five   nine   one   seven   two   _____

Thoughts:

Hopefully you were successful with the shift from the number to the language-based set. If not, you should expand the language-based possibilities to include an alphabetically based set. Try again and pay particular attention to the first letter in each word. When you solve the problem or exhaust all your solutions, turn to the next page.

Eight   five   nine   one   seven   two   _____

Thoughts:

As you may or may not have detected, the puzzle follows an ascending alphabetical progression from "E" to "T." The next number in the sequence is "zero."

Now that you are aware of the obstacles mental sets present, you should try to expand, rather than limit, your approach to problems. How can you counteract their effects in other aspects of your life?

Reference

Bransford, J. D., & Johnson, M. K. (1972). Contextual prerequisites for understanding: Some investigations of comprehension and recall. *Journal of Verbal Learning and Verbal Behavior, 11,* 717-726.

Name _____

Active Learning Experience

3.2 Heuristics

Before reading further, follow the directions below.

For the causes of death listed in each comparison, check which cause of death occurs more frequently in the United States.

Suicide _____ vs. Homicide _____

Breast Cancer _____ vs. Diabetes _____

Stroke _____ vs. All Accidents _____

Appendicitis _____ vs. Pregnancy, abortion, child birth _____

This activity is based on research by Baruch Fisckhoff, Paul Slovic, and Sarah Lichtenstein (1977). If you checked *homicide, breast cancer, all accidents,* and *pregnancy, abortion and child birth*, you would be responding similarly to most subjects in their study. Unfortunately, you would also be wrong. Not only did the majority of subjects choose each of these alternatives, they were very confident in their decisions.

The authors accounted for this behavior by noting that each of these choices "is a dramatic, well-publicized event, whereas the [other cause] is a more 'quiet' killer... In these cases, people may be relying on the greater availability in memory of examples of the 'flashier' causes of death without realizing that availability is an imperfect inferential rule" (p 563).

This phenomenon is referred to as the availability heuristic. Because certain events are more newsworthy, they are given disproportionate attention by the media. Therefore, instances of their occurrence are more easily recalled.

How might this phenomenon affect your decision making in other situations?

Reference

Fisckhoff, B., Slovic, P., & Lichtenstein, S. (1977). Knowing with certainty: The appropriateness of extreme confidence. *Journal of Experimental Psychology: Human Perception and Performance, 3*, 552-564.

Name _____

Active Learning Experience

3.3 Actor-Observer Phenomenon

Before reading further, complete the following task.

On the questionnaire below, look at the choices in *each row* and indicate which of the three choices seems most appropriate as a description of you.   For example, would you describe yourself as "serious" or "easy going," or does it "depend on the situation"? Put a check in front of the most appropriate response. ***Please do this for each of the twenty rows (one choice for each row).***

Self

1.	_____ Serious	_____ Easy going	_____ Depends on the situation
2.	_____ Spontaneous	_____ Analytical	_____ Depends on the situation
3.	_____ Imaginative	_____ Down to earth	_____ Depends on the situation
4.	_____ Energetic	_____ Relaxed	_____ Depends on the situation
5.	_____ Unassuming	_____ Self-asserting	_____ Depends on the situation
6.	_____ Lenient	_____ Rigorous	_____ Depends on the situation
7.	_____ Unemotional	_____ Emotional	_____ Depends on the situation
8.	_____ Formal	_____ Casual	_____ Depends on the situation
9.	_____ Realistic	_____ Idealistic	_____ Depends on the situation
10.	_____ Intense	_____ Calm	_____ Depends on the situation
11.	_____ Cynical	_____ Gullible	_____ Depends on the situation
12.	_____ Quiet	_____ Talkative	_____ Depends on the situation
13.	_____ Active	_____ Passive	_____ Depends on the situation
14.	_____ Soft-hearted	_____ Tough-minded	_____ Depends on the situation
15.	_____ Task oriented	_____ People oriented	_____ Depends on the situation
16.	_____ Firm	_____ Flexible	_____ Depends on the situation

17. _____ Proud _____ Humble _____ Depends on the situation

18. _____ Cautious _____ Daring _____ Depends on the situation

19. _____ Uninhibited _____ Self-controlled _____ Depends on the situation

20. _____ Conscientious _____ Carefree _____ Depends on the situation

Think of a well known TV personality. On the questionnaire below, look at the choices in *each row* and indicate which of the three choices seems most appropriate as a description for that person. For example, would you describe this person as "serious" or "easy going," or does it "depend on the situation"? Put a check in front of the most appropriate response. ***Please do this for each of the twenty rows (one choice for each row).***

Name of person rated _____

1. _____ Serious _____ Easy going _____ Depends on the situation

2. _____ Spontaneous _____ Analytical _____ Depends on the situation

3. _____ Imaginative _____ Down to earth _____ Depends on the situation

4. _____ Energetic _____ Relaxed _____ Depends on the situation

5. _____ Unassuming _____ Self-asserting _____ Depends on the situation

6. _____ Lenient _____ Rigorous _____ Depends on the situation

7. _____ Unemotional _____ Emotional _____ Depends on the situation

8. _____ Formal _____ Casual _____ Depends on the situation

9. _____ Realistic _____ Idealistic _____ Depends on the situation

10. _____ Intense _____ Calm _____ Depends on the situation

11. _____ Cynical _____ Gullible _____ Depends on the situation

12. _____ Quiet _____ Talkative _____ Depends on the situation

13. _____ Active _____ Passive _____ Depends on the situation

14. _____ Soft-hearted _____ Tough-minded _____ Depends on the situation

15. _____ Task oriented _____ People oriented _____ Depends on the situation

16. _____ Firm   _____ Flexible   _____ Depends on the situation

17. _____ Proud   _____ Humble   _____ Depends on the situation

18. _____ Cautious   _____ Daring   _____ Depends on the situation

19. _____ Uninhibited   _____ Self-controlled   _____ Depends on the situation

20. _____ Conscientious   _____ Carefree   _____ Depends on the situation

Richard Nisbett and several associates (1973) conducted an experiment that involved a task similar to the one you completed. It was designed to test the actor-observer phenomenon--people view the causes of others' behavior differently than they view the causes of their own behavior. More specifically, actors tend to view their own behavior in relation to situational factors, while observers tend to view others' behaviors as manifestations of their personal dispositions or qualities. In the present experiment, they indeed found a significant difference in the number of *personality traits* ascribed to themselves as opposed to others. Participants were more likely to choose the "depends-on-the-situation" category for themselves than for others. How did you do? (count the number of times you circled depends-on-the-situation for yourself and the person you rated)?

Self _____   Other _____

Have you noticed this phenomenon in other situations? Describe one.

What are the ramifications of this phenomenon for our everyday encounters with people?

How is it adaptive?

How is it problematic?

Reference

Nisbett, R. E., Caputo, C., Legant, P., & Marecek, J. (1973). Behavior as seen by the actor and as seen by the observer. *Journal of Personality and Social Psychology, 27,* 154-164.

CHAPTER 4

Attitudes and Persuasion

Name _____

Active Learning Experience

4.1 Attitudes and Behavior

Attitude Survey

Indicate the extent to which you agree or disagree with each of the five statements by using the following scale:

> 1 = strongly disagree
> 2 = disagree
> 3 = no opinion
> 4 = agree
> 5 = strongly agree

_____ 1. The use of seatbelts saves lives.

_____ 2. Exposure to the sun's ultraviolet rays can cause skin cancer.

_____ 3. Eating a low-fat diet is beneficial to one's health.

_____ 4. Sexually transmitted diseases can be prevented.

_____ 5. Recycling is important to preserve the environment.

Now complete the "Behavior Survey" below by circling the appropriate answer.

Behavior Survey

yes   no   1.   I always use a seatbelt.

yes   no   2.   I use the appropriate sunscreen whenever I go outside.

yes   no   3.   I maintain a low-fat diet.

yes   no   4.   I always practice safe sex.

yes   no   5.   I recycle cans, bottles, and paper.

This adaptation of a procedure developed by David Carkenoid and Joseph Bullington (1993) is designed to help you understand the relationship between attitudes and behaviors.

In comparing your attitudes and your behaviors, are there any discrepancies (e.g., "strongly agreeing" or "agreeing" with an attitude statement and responding "no" to the corresponding behavior?

When we encounter discrepancies between our attitudes and behaviors, we are likely to experience "cognitive dissonance"--a motivating force to change either an attitude or behavior. When we reconcile the discrepancy, we reduce dissonance. If you noted any discrepancies in this task, how do (did) you reconcile them?

From your experience, describe a situation in which you felt strong dissonance to change an attitude or behavior. What did you do?

Reference

Carkenoid, D. M., & Bullington, J. (1993). Bringing cognitive dissonance to the classroom. *Teaching of Psychology, 20*, 41-43.

Name _____

Active Learning Experience

4.2 Ad Analysis

To gain a clearer understanding of communication and the importance of the *message, the messenger, how the message is communicated*, and the *intended audience*, analyze five ads (each from a different magazine, preferably diverse magazines).

1.   Magazine _____

Brief description of ad.

How effective is this ad? Why

2.   Magazine _____

Brief description of ad.

How effective is this ad? Why

3.   Magazine _____

Brief description of ad.

How effective is this ad? Why

4.　Magazine _____

Brief description of ad.

How effective is this ad? Why

5.　Magazine _____

Brief description of ad.

How effective is this ad? Why

62

Based on what you have learned about the importance of the four elements of communication, design an ad for a product of your choice.

Product -

Intended Audience -

Messenger -

Message -

How communicated -

Name _____

Active Learning Experience

4.3 Need for Cognition

Before reading further, answer the following questions on the 5-point scale.

1. I really enjoy a task that involves coming up with new solutions to problems.

1	2	3	4	5
Extremely Uncharacteristic of Me	Somewhat Uncharacteristic of Me	Uncertain	Somewhat Characteristic of Me	Extremely Characteristic of Me

2. I would prefer a task that is intellectual, difficult, and important to one that is somewhat important but does not require much thought.

1	2	3	4	5
Extremely Uncharacteristic of Me	Somewhat Uncharacteristic of Me	Uncertain	Somewhat Characteristic of Me	Extremely Characteristic of Me

3. I tend to set goals that can be accomplished only by expending considerable mental effort.

1	2	3	4	5
Extremely Uncharacteristic of Me	Somewhat Uncharacteristic of Me	Uncertain	Somewhat Characteristic of Me	Extremely Characteristic of Me

4. I am usually tempted to put more thought into a task than the job minimally requires.

1	2	3	4	5
Extremely Uncharacteristic of Me	Somewhat Uncharacteristic of Me	Uncertain	Somewhat Characteristic of Me	Extremely Characteristic of Me

5. Learning new ways to think doesn't excite me very much.

1	2	3	4	5
Extremely Uncharacteristic of Me	Somewhat Uncharacteristic of Me	Uncertain	Somewhat Characteristic of Me	Extremely Characteristic of Me

6. I am hesitant about making important decisions after thinking about them.

1	2	3	4	5
Extremely Uncharacteristic of Me	Somewhat Uncharacteristic of Me	Uncertain	Somewhat Characteristic of Me	Extremely Characteristic of Me

7. I usually end up deliberating about issues even when they do not affect me personally.

1	2	3	4	5
Extremely Uncharacteristic of Me	Somewhat Uncharacteristic of Me	Uncertain	Somewhat Characteristic of Me	Extremely Characteristic of Me

8. I prefer just to let things happen rather than try to understand why they turned out that way.

1	2	3	4	5
Extremely Uncharacteristic of Me	Somewhat Uncharacteristic of Me	Uncertain	Somewhat Characteristic of Me	Extremely Characteristic of Me

9. I have difficulty thinking in new and unfamiliar situations.

1	2	3	4	5
Extremely Uncharacteristic of Me	Somewhat Uncharacteristic of Me	Uncertain	Somewhat Characteristic of Me	Extremely Characteristic of Me

10. The idea of relying on thought to make my way to the top does not appeal to me.

1	2	3	4	5
Extremely Uncharacteristic of Me	Somewhat Uncharacteristic of Me	Uncertain	Somewhat Characteristic of Me	Extremely Characteristic of Me

11. The notion of thinking abstractly is not appealing to me.

1	2	3	4	5
Extremely Uncharacteristic of Me	Somewhat Uncharacteristic of Me	Uncertain	Somewhat Characteristic of Me	Extremely Characteristic of Me

12. I am an intellectual.

1	2	3	4	5
Extremely Uncharacteristic of Me	Somewhat Uncharacteristic of Me	Uncertain	Somewhat Characteristic of Me	Extremely Characteristic of Me

13. I only think as hard as I have to.

1	2	3	4	5
Extremely Uncharacteristic of Me	Somewhat Uncharacteristic of Me	Uncertain	Somewhat Characteristic of Me	Extremely Characteristic of Me

14. I don't reason well under pressure.

1	2	3	4	5
Extremely Uncharacteristic of Me	Somewhat Uncharacteristic of Me	Uncertain	Somewhat Characteristic of Me	Extremely Characteristic of Me

15. I like tasks that require little thought once I've learned them.

1	2	3	4	5
Extremely Uncharacteristic of Me	Somewhat Uncharacteristic of Me	Uncertain	Somewhat Characteristic of Me	Extremely Characteristic of Me

16. I prefer to think about small, daily projects to long-term ones.

1	2	3	4	5
Extremely Uncharacteristic of Me	Somewhat Uncharacteristic of Me	Uncertain	Somewhat Characteristic of Me	Extremely Characteristic of Me

17. I would rather do something that requires little thought than something that is sure to challenge my thinking abilities.

1	2	3	4	5
Extremely Uncharacteristic of Me	Somewhat Uncharacteristic of Me	Uncertain	Somewhat Characteristic of Me	Extremely Characteristic of Me

18. I find little satisfaction in deliberating hard and for long hours.

1	2	3	4	5
Extremely Uncharacteristic of Me	Somewhat Uncharacteristic of Me	Uncertain	Somewhat Characteristic of Me	Extremely Characteristic of Me

19. I more often talk with other people about the reasons for and possible solutions to international problems than about gossip or tidbits of what famous people are doing.

1	2	3	4	5
Extremely Uncharacteristic of Me	Somewhat Uncharacteristic of Me	Uncertain	Somewhat Characteristic of Me	Extremely Characteristic of Me

20. These days, I see little chance for performing well, even in "intellectual" jobs, unless one knows the right people.

1	2	3	4	5
Extremely Uncharacteristic of Me	Somewhat Uncharacteristic of Me	Uncertain	Somewhat Characteristic of Me	Extremely Characteristic of Me

21. More often than not, more thinking just leads to more errors.

1	2	3	4	5
Extremely Uncharacteristic of Me	Somewhat Uncharacteristic of Me	Uncertain	Somewhat Characteristic of Me	Extremely Characteristic of Me

22. I don't like to have the responsibility of handling a situation that requires a lot of thinking.

1	2	3	4	5
Extremely Uncharacteristic of Me	Somewhat Uncharacteristic of Me	Uncertain	Somewhat Characteristic of Me	Extremely Characteristic of Me

23. I appreciate opportunities to discover the strengths and weaknesses of my own reasoning.

1	2	3	4	5
Extremely Uncharacteristic of Me	Somewhat Uncharacteristic of Me	Uncertain	Somewhat Characteristic of Me	Extremely Characteristic of Me

24. I feel relief rather than satisfaction after completing a task that required a lot of mental effort.

1	2	3	4	5
Extremely Uncharacteristic of Me	Somewhat Uncharacteristic of Me	Uncertain	Somewhat Characteristic of Me	Extremely Characteristic of Me

25. Thinking is not my idea of fun.

1	2	3	4	5
Extremely Uncharacteristic of Me	Somewhat Uncharacteristic of Me	Uncertain	Somewhat Characteristic of Me	Extremely Characteristic of Me

26. I try to anticipate and avoid situations where there is a likely chance I will have to think in depth about something.

1	2	3	4	5
Extremely Uncharacteristic of Me	Somewhat Uncharacteristic of Me	Uncertain	Somewhat Characteristic of Me	Extremely Characteristic of Me

27. I prefer watching educational to entertainment programs.

1	2	3	4	5
Extremely Uncharacteristic of Me	Somewhat Uncharacteristic of Me	Uncertain	Somewhat Characteristic of Me	Extremely Characteristic of Me

28. I think best when those around me are very intelligent.

1	2	3	4	5
Extremely Uncharacteristic of Me	Somewhat Uncharacteristic of Me	Uncertain	Somewhat Characteristic of Me	Extremely Characteristic of Me

29. I prefer my life to be filled with puzzles that I must solve.

1	2	3	4	5
Extremely Uncharacteristic of Me	Somewhat Uncharacteristic of Me	Uncertain	Somewhat Characteristic of Me	Extremely Characteristic of Me

30. I would prefer complex to simple problems.

1	2	3	4	5
Extremely Uncharacteristic of Me	Somewhat Uncharacteristic of Me	Uncertain	Somewhat Characteristic of Me	Extremely Characteristic of Me

31. Simply knowing the answer rather than understanding the reasons for the answer to a problem is fine with me.

1	2	3	4	5
Extremely Uncharacteristic of Me	Somewhat Uncharacteristic of Me	Uncertain	Somewhat Characteristic of Me	Extremely Characteristic of Me

68

32. It's enough for me that something gets the job done, I don't care how or why it works.

1	2	3	4	5
Extremely Uncharacteristic of Me	Somewhat Uncharacteristic of Me	Uncertain	Somewhat Characteristic of Me	Extremely Characteristic of Me

33. Ignorance is bliss.

1	2	3	4	5
Extremely Uncharacteristic of Me	Somewhat Uncharacteristic of Me	Uncertain	Somewhat Characteristic of Me	Extremely Characteristic of Me

34. I enjoy thinking about an issue even when the results of my thought will have no effect on the outcome of the issue.

1	2	3	4	5
Extremely Uncharacteristic of Me	Somewhat Uncharacteristic of Me	Uncertain	Somewhat Characteristic of Me	Extremely Characteristic of Me

From Cacioppo, J. T., & Petty, R. E. (1980). The need for cognition. *Journal of Personality and Social Psychology, 42*, 116-131. Copyright © 1980 by the American Psychological Association. Reprinted with permission.

Scoring

Add the scores for all items after reversing the scores (e.g., 5 = 1, 4 = 2, 3 = 3, 2 = 4, 1 = 5) on the following items: 5, 6, 8, 9, 10, 11, 13, 14, 15, 16, 17, 18, 20, 21, 22, 24, 25, 26, 31, 32, and 33.

Total score = _____

John Cacioppo and Richard Petty (1980) developed this scale to assess individuals' "tendency to engage in and enjoy thinking." (p. 116). I have found a mean of 117 and a standard deviation of 16 for this scale. This "need for cognition" has been found to predict people's behavior in a variety of situations. However, with respect to attitude change and persuasion, those high in need for cognition are more responsive to central as opposed to peripheral messages (Cacioppo, Petty, Feinstein, and Jarvis, 1996).

Describe recent attempts by others to influence or persuade you. What routes were used? Which attempts were most successful?

References

Cacioppo, J. T., & Petty, R. E. (1980). The need for cognition. *Journal of Personality and Social Psychology, 42*, 116-131.

Cacioppo, J. T., Petty, R. E., Feinstein, J. A., & Jarvis, W. B. G. (1996). Dispositional differences in cognitive motivation: The life and times of individuals varying in need for cognition. *Psychological Bulletin, 119*, 197-253.

CHAPTER 5

Conformity

Name _____

Active Learning Experience

5.1 Norms

Marianne Misirandino (1992) described an interesting way to illustrate attitudes toward studying. The following activity is an adaptation of her procedures.

For the purpose of this activity, it is assumed that you are a full-time student. If not, prorate your estimates to the following questions. For example, if you are a half-time student, multiply your estimates by 2. If you are a one-third time student, multiply your estimate by 3. And so on.

1. How many hours a *week* do you typically study? _____

2. What would you consider the *ideal* number of hours a week to study? _____

3. What is the lowest number of hours a week to study that you would consider tolerable? _____

4. What is the highest number of hours a week to study that you would consider tolerable? _____

Turn in your individual results to your instructor, who will calculate means for your class for each of the four questions.

What were your class means for studying behavior?

1. typical   _____

2. ideal   _____

3. lowest tolerable   _____

4. highest tolerable _____

The number of hours between #3 and #4 represents the range of tolerable studying behavior, and may be considered the norm for your college.

How does your typical number of hours spent studying a week fit with this norm?

What kinds of pressure might be felt by those who deviate from the norm, in either direction?

Given this normative information, are you motivated to change your studying behavior in any way? Explain.

Describe other norms that operate in your class. What pressures are exerted to conform? How are deviations dealt with? What do you think of these norms?

Reference

Misirandino, M. (1992). Studying a social norm. *Teaching of Psychology, 19*, 103-106.

Name _____

Active Learning Experience

5.2 Social Influence

This activity, based on the research of Glenn White (1975) and a demonstration by Neil Lutsky (1993), will give you a chance to conduct an experiment on social influence. The method involves asking subjects to respond to a survey on "How much students should be expected to spend on textbooks per course." There will be three conditions. Condition one will have eight lines filled with names and amounts averaging $35.00. Condition two will have eight lines filled with names and amounts averaging $90.00. Condition three will have no names or amounts, just blank lines.

For Condition one, ask your classmates to fill in their names on the first eight lines and assign one of the following amounts for each to fill in above his/her name: $30; $35; $25; $40; $45; $25; $35; $45. For Condition two, also solicit help from your classmates for names and the following amounts: $90; $80; $100; $85; $95; $75; $100; $95. This way, it will look like actual survey sheets with real names and amounts in different handwriting.

Recruit three people, at different times, to respond to the survey. In Conditions one and two, they will be the ninth respondents, and in condition three, the first respondent. Before conducting the survey, cut off the heading and page number at the top of each form.

As with any experiment, be sure to follow the guidelines for research imposed by your school, and debrief your subjects when the research has been completed.

Once you collect your data, you can combine your results with your classmates. Appropriate analyses can be conducted, and you can determine the significance of the findings.

Survey

We are conducting a survey of student opinions regarding the maximum amount that a student should be expected to pay for the books required for **each course**. Please express your estimates in dollars.

Name   Amount

1. _____

2. _____

3. _____

4. _____

5. _____

6. _____

7. _____

8. _____

9. _____

10. _____

11. _____

12. _____

13. _____

14. _____

15. _____

16. _____

17. _____

18. _____

19. _____

20. _____

Survey

We are conducting a survey of student opinions regarding the maximum amount that a student should be expected to pay for the books required for **each course**. Please express your estimates in dollars.

Name   Amount

1. _____

2. _____

3. _____

4. _____

5. _____

6. _____

7. _____

8. _____

9. _____

10. _____

11. _____

12. _____

13. _____

14. _____

15. _____

16. _____

17. _____

18. _____

19. _____

20. _____

Survey

We are conducting a survey of student opinions regarding the maximum amount that a student should be expected to pay for the books required for **each course**. Please express your estimates in dollars.

Name   Amount

1. _____

2. _____

3. _____

4. _____

5. _____

6. _____

7. _____

8. _____

9. _____

10. _____

11. _____

12. _____

13. _____

14. _____

15. _____

16. _____

17. _____

18. _____

19. _____

20. _____

Does this form of social influence have an effect on subjects? Explain.

References

Lutsky, N. (1993). A scheme and variations for studies of social influence in an experimental social psychology laboratory. *Teaching of Psychology, 20,* 105-107.

White, G. M. (1975). Contextual determinants of opinion judgments: Field experimental probes of judgmental relativity boundary conditions. *Journal of Personality and Social Psychology, 32,* 1047-1054.

Name _____

Active Learning Experience

5.3 Conformity and Non Conformity

Describe a time when you conformed to social pressure. What factors influenced you the most?

Describe a time when you violated a social norm. How did others react to you? What were your thoughts and feelings?

Describe a time when you actively resisted social pressure. How did others react to you? What were your thoughts and feelings?

Taken together, these experiences demonstrate the power of norms and social influence. The third part of this activity emphasizes the power of the individual. It also highlights the importance of personal freedom (especially when it is threatened) and individual uniqueness. People often get caught up in being like everyone else and doing what everyone else does, to the point where individual uniqueness is compromised. However, we should never lose sight of our "selves."

CHAPTER 6

Behavior in Groups

88

Active Learning Experience

6.1 Deindividuation

This task should be done anonymously.

Before reading further, respond to this question: "If you could do anything humanly possible with complete assurance that you would not be detected or held responsible, what would you do?" (Dodd, 1985, p. 90).

Describe your thoughts and feelings while you completed this task.

David Dodd (1985) asked this question in several of his classes to illustrate deindividuation–the process of losing one's sense of personal identity that may result in behaviors that deviate from the norm. In this case, behaviors that are usually inhibited are released!

Dodd demonstrated clearly that "even 'normal, well-adjusted' college students are capable of highly inappropriate, antisocial behavior, given certain social and situational conditions (1985, p. 87). He found that 36% of the responses were *antisocial* (injuring others or depriving others of their rights) and 19% were *nonnormative* (violating social norms and practices). With respect to specific behaviors, 26% involved criminal acts, 11% involved sexual acts, and 11% involved spying behaviors. Nine percent of the responses were *prosocial* (benefiting others).

How did the results of your class compare with these statistics?

In what situations have you observed deindividuation occurring? Describe the specific behaviors you noted.

Reference

Dodd, D. K. (1985). Robbers in the classroom: A deindividuation exercise. *Teaching of Psychology, 12,* 89-91.

Name _____

Active Learning Experience

6.2 Risk Decisions

Read the scenarios below and follow the instructions for each one.

1. Amy is 35 years old and looking to invest her life savings for her retirement. She is considering options to buy two different stocks. One of the stocks has a long history of small but steady growth. It is considered to be a conservative, low risk investment. The other stock is new on the market. Although it holds potential for rapid growth, it also has the potential to fail, producing large losses. It's considered to be an aggressive, high risk investment.

In advising Amy, check the lowest probability of success that you would consider acceptable for her to buy the riskier stock.

_____ The likelihood is 1 in 10 that it will be successful.

_____ The likelihood is 2 in 10 that it will be successful.

_____ The likelihood is 3 in 10 that it will be successful.

_____ The likelihood is 4 in 10 that it will be successful.

_____ The likelihood is 5 in 10 that it will be successful.

_____ The likelihood is 6 in 10 that it will be successful.

_____ The likelihood is 7 in 10 that it will be successful.

_____ The likelihood is 8 in 10 that it will be successful.

_____ The likelihood is 9 in 10 that it will be successful.

_____ The likelihood is 10 in 10 that it will be successful.

2. Mary is a college senior who has received two job offers. One of the jobs is with a high paying, prestigious corporation that hires a large number of entry level people. However, there is intense competition among employees for a small number of promotions. As a result, many will be terminated after one year. The other corporation does not pay as well and does not have nearly as prestigious a reputation, but they hire a small number of employees and are committed to seeing them move up the ranks.

In advising Mary, check the lowest probability of success that you would consider acceptable for her to take the more prestigious job.

_____ The likelihood is 1 in 10 that it will be successful.

_____ The likelihood is 2 in 10 that it will be successful.

_____ The likelihood is 3 in 10 that it will be successful.

_____ The likelihood is 4 in 10 that it will be successful.

_____ The likelihood is 5 in 10 that it will be successful.

_____ The likelihood is 6 in 10 that it will be successful.

_____ The likelihood is 7 in 10 that it will be successful.

_____ The likelihood is 8 in 10 that it will be successful.

_____ The likelihood is 9 in 10 that it will be successful.

_____ The likelihood is 10 in 10 that it will be successful.

3. John is playing in the final match for the state golf championship. He and his opponent are tied after 17 holes. On the 18th, and final, hole his opponent hits his tee shot safely onto the green, about 35 feet from the hole. He has a difficult putt and will likely need two strokes to get into the hole for a par 3. John has a decision to make. He can try to hit his tee shot onto the safe part of the green, near his opponent, and likely get a par 3 to send the match to extra holes to determine the winner, or he can try a riskier shot directly at the hole. If successful, he would have an excellent chance to win the hole and the match with a 2. However, this area of the green is surrounded by a water hazard. If his shot is off line, he will likely go into the hazard and lose the hole and the match.

In advising John, check the lowest probability of success that you would consider acceptable for him to take the riskier shot.

_____ The likelihood is 1 in 10 that it will be successful.

_____ The likelihood is 2 in 10 that it will be successful.

_____ The likelihood is 3 in 10 that it will be successful.

_____ The likelihood is 4 in 10 that it will be successful.

_____ The likelihood is 5 in 10 that it will be successful.

_____ The likelihood is 6 in 10 that it will be successful.

_____ The likelihood is 7 in 10 that it will be successful.

_____ The likelihood is 8 in 10 that it will be successful.

_____ The likelihood is 9 in 10 that it will be successful.

_____ The likelihood is 10 in 10 that it will be successful.

96

Your instructor will assign you to a group and provide additional copies of the scenarios for you to consider. Discussion should end when a unanimous group decision (or if one does not occur, a majority vote) on the *lowest* probability of success required to choose the riskier option has been made for each scenario.

Do not read further until instructed to do so.

Describe the group discussion of each topic. For example, were factors you did not consider expressed?

1. (Stocks)

2. (Job)

3.   (Golf)

What are your thoughts and feelings about the final decisions?

1.   (Stocks)

2.   (Jobs)

3.   (Golf)

What was the probability level that your group arrived at for each scenario:

    1. (Stocks) - _____

    2. (Job) - _____

    3. (Golf) - _____

Was there a difference between your initial decision and the group's decision (you should also examine the results for other group members and groups)? What conclusion can you draw from the experience?

This experiment is based on the research of Kogan and Wallach (1964) and an activity developed by Goethals and Demorest (1979) on group polarization. What frequently occurs in groups is a movement toward *greater* caution or risk (depending on the initial inclinations of individuals in the groups) following group discussions. Can you relate this to other situations you may have encountered?

References

Goethals, G. R., & Demorest, A. P. (1979). The risky shift is a sure bet. *Teaching of Psychology, 6,* 177-179.

Kogan, N., & Wallach, M. A. (1964). *Risk taking: A study in cognition and personality.* New York: Holt, Rinehart, and Winston.

Name _____

Active Learning Experience

6.3 Prisoner's Dilemma

Try to envision the following scenario as vividly as possible.

You and another suspect in a major crime are arrested and brought to separate rooms for questioning by the district attorney. You are both guilty, but the district attorney has only enough evidence to convict the two of you of a lesser offense.

Given this situation, the district attorney offers the following plea bargain to each of you privately: If one of you confesses to the major crime and the other does not, the district attorney will grant the confessor immunity (and use the confession to convict the other of this major crime, which carries a 15 year sentence). If both of you confess, each will receive a moderate sentence (5 years). If neither confesses, each of you will receive a light sentence for the lesser offense (1 year).

	You Confess	You Don't Confess
Other Confesses	You get 5 years / Other gets 5 years	You get 15 years / Other gets 0 years
Other Doesn't Confess	You get 0 years / Other gets 15 years	You get 1 year / Other gets 1 year

What would you do? Explain.

This is an example of a social dilemma, a conflict situation referred to as the Prisoner's Dilemma. Although this example involves the legal system, many other day to day decisions require solutions that impact others. While we frequently want the best solution for ourselves and the other party, to accomplish this, each person must *trust* the other. And this is when the problem frequently arises. Do we trust the other person and do we think he or she trusts us? Many people in this situation choose to confess.

Given the same scenario, with one change--*neither of you is guilty* of the major crime, what would you do? Explain your reasoning.

What would you do if you were innocent of the major crime and the other suspect was guilty? Explain.

Describe a situation you have faced that involves this type of dilemma. How did you resolve it?

CHAPTER 7

Stereotyping, Prejudice, and Discrimination

Name _____

Active Learning Experience

7.1 Character Analysis

As you read the following vignette, visualize the scene. Try to see the participants as vividly as possible.

Terry desired Chris and frequently imagined the two of them making love. Terry envisioned them lying naked, kissing, their bodies entwined, moving rhythmically together. When they were together on dates, Terry pushed to move the relationship to this next level.

Chris did not see their relationship the same way. Terry was a fun date, but Chris was worried that things were moving too fast. Chris wanted to get to know Terry much better before having sex. But sex was becoming a source of conflict between them. They were clearly two people with different perspectives on their relationship.

Respond to the following questions about the principal characters.

Who was more fun-loving?--

Who was more spontaneous?--

Who was more conservative?--

Who was more adventurous?--

Who was more passionate?--

Who was more complex?--

Who was more vulnerable?--

How old do you envision Chris to be?--

How old do you envision Terry to be?--

What is Chris's gender?--

What is Terry's gender?--

Were the questions difficult for you to answer? If so, which ones were most difficult?
Why?

The easier this task (based on a story from Baumeister and Tice, 2001, p. 95) was for you, the more likely you are prone to stereotyped thinking about gender, age, and relationships. If, on the other hand, you considered a variety of possibilities for the genders of Chris and Terry (i.e., Chris, male; Terry, female; Chris, female, Terry, male; Chris, female, Terry, female; Chris male, Terry, male) and a range of age possibilities, you may be a more open-minded thinker.

Reference

Baumeister, R. F., & Tice, D. M. (2001). *The social dimension of sex*. Boston: Allyn & Bacon.

Name _____

Active Learning Experience

7.2 Prejudice

Before reading further, react to each of the following statements using the seven point scale, from strongly disagree to strongly agree.

1. In today's society it is important that one not be perceived as prejudiced in any manner.

-3	-2	-1	0	+1	+2	+3
Strongly Disagree						Strongly Agree

2. I get angry with myself when I have a thought or feeling that might be considered prejudiced.

-3	-2	-1	0	+1	+2	+3
Strongly Disagree						Strongly Agree

3. It's important to me that other people not think I'm prejudiced.

-3	-2	-1	0	+1	+2	+3
Strongly Disagree						Strongly Agree

4. It's never acceptable to express one's prejudices.

-3	-2	-1	0	+1	+2	+3
Strongly Disagree						Strongly Agree

5. I feel guilty when I have a negative thought or feeling about a [person of a different race].

-3	-2	-1	0	+1	+2	+3
Strongly Disagree						Strongly Agree

6. When speaking to a [person of a difference race], it's important to me that he/she not think I'm prejudiced.

-3	-2	-1	0	+1	+2	+3
Strongly Disagree						Strongly Agree

7. It bothers me a great deal when I think I've offended someone, so I'm always careful to consider other people's feelings.

-3	-2	-1	0	+1	+2	+3
Strongly Disagree						Strongly Agree

8. If I have a prejudiced thought or feeling, I keep it to myself.

-3	-2	-1	0	+1	+2	+3
Strongly Disagree						Strongly Agree

9. I would never tell jokes that might offend others.

-3	-2	-1	0	+1	+2	+3
Strongly Disagree						Strongly Agree

From Dunton, B. C., & Fazio, R. H. (1997). An individual difference measure of motivation to control prejudiced reactions. *Personality and Social Psychology Bulletin, 23,* 316-326. Copyright © 1997 by Sage Publications, Inc. Reprinted with permission.

Scoring

Total your score on all items and divide by nine.

Score _____

This is a slightly modified version of the "concern with acting prejudiced" factor of Bridget Dunton and Russell Fazio's (1997) Motivation to Control Prejudiced Reactions Scale. It contains "items that reflect being concerned about appearing prejudiced to others," "ones that reflect a more private concern with observing oneself having prejudiced thoughts or feelings," "and ones that reflect a personal standard regarding the avoidance of prejudice and offensive expressions" (pp. 320-321).

You can estimate the strength of your motivation to either control or express prejudice by how far your score deviates from zero. Positive scores indicate motivation to control prejudice. How would you interpret your score?

114

Describe your own behavior in relation to this scale.

Reference

Dunton, B. C., & Fazio, R. H. (1997). An individual difference measure of motivation to control prejudiced reactions. *Personality and Social Psychology Bulletin, 23*, 316-326.

Name _____

Active Learning Experience

7.3 Discrimination

While prejudice is an attitude, discrimination is a behavior. Blatant forms of discrimination, based on gender, race, ethnicity, religious preference, and sexual orientation, are well documented, but even those who have never suffered for these reasons may experience discrimination. People and institutions discriminate for many other reasons, such as age, height, weight, appearance, marital status, education, social economic level, occupation, etc.

Describe a time when you felt that you were discriminated against. What did you think and how did you feel?

Patricia Devine (1995) described the difficulty we have in trying to eliminate prejudice and discriminatory behavior. A decision "to renounce prejudice [does] not immediately eliminate [discrimination] ... That is, overcoming prejudice requires overcoming a lifetime of socialization experiences. (p. 173). She likens the process to breaking a bad habit. Plus, we frequently "encounter situations in which there is pressure from other people to respond in ways that conflict with [our] personal standards." (p. 173). "It takes conscious attention, energy, and effort" (p. 173).

Describe a time when you felt you discriminated against someone.

What can individuals do to reduce prejudice and eliminate discrimination?

Reference

Devine, P. G. (1995). Getting hooked on research in social psychology: Examples from eyewitness identification and prejudice. In G. G. Brannigan & M. R. Merrens (Eds.), *The social psychologists: Research adventures*, Boston: McGraw-Hill.

CHAPTER 8

Aggression

Name _____

Active Learning Experience

8.1 Aggression Scale

Respond to each of the following questions on the five point scale.

1. There are people who pushed me so far that we came to blows.

   1   2   3   4   5

   Extremely   Extremely
   Uncharacteristic of Me   *Characteristic* of Me

2. I tell my friends openly when I disagree with them.

   1   2   3   4   5

   Extremely   Extremely
   Uncharacteristic of Me   *Characteristic* of Me

3. I am sometimes eaten up with jealousy.

   1   2   3   4   5

   Extremely   Extremely
   Uncharacteristic of Me   *Characteristic* of Me

4. I sometimes feel like a powder keg ready to explode.

   1   2   3   4   5

   Extremely   Extremely
   Uncharacteristic of Me   *Characteristic* of Me

5. Once in a while I can't control the urge to strike another person.

   1   2   3   4   5

   Extremely   Extremely
   Uncharacteristic of Me   *Characteristic* of Me

6. When people annoy me, I may tell them what I think of them.

   1   2   3   4   5

   Extremely   Extremely
   Uncharacteristic of Me   *Characteristic* of Me

7. I wonder why sometimes I feel so bitter about things.

1	2	3	4	5

    Extremely
    Uncharacteristic of Me

    Extremely
    Characteristic of Me

8. I flare up quickly but get over it quickly.

1	2	3	4	5

    Extremely
    Uncharacteristic of Me

    Extremely
    Characteristic of Me

9. Given enough provocation, I may hit another person.

1	2	3	4	5

    Extremely
    Uncharacteristic of Me

    Extremely
    Characteristic of Me

10. When people are especially nice, I wonder what they want.

1	2	3	4	5

    Extremely
    Uncharacteristic of Me

    Extremely
    Characteristic of Me

11. Sometimes I fly off the handle for no good reason.

1	2	3	4	5

    Extremely
    Uncharacteristic of Me

    Extremely
    Characteristic of Me

12. My friends say that I'm somewhat argumentative.

1	2	3	4	5

    Extremely
    Uncharacteristic of Me

    Extremely
    Characteristic of Me

13. If I have to resort to violence to protect my rights, I will.

1	2	3	4	5

    Extremely
    Uncharacteristic of Me

    Extremely
    Characteristic of Me

14. I have become so mad that I have broken things.

1	2	3	4	5

    Extremely
    Uncharacteristic of Me

    Extremely
    Characteristic of Me

15. I am suspicious of overly friendly strangers.

       1   2   3   4   5

Extremely   Extremely

Uncharacteristic of Me   *Characteristic* of Me

16. Other people always seem to get the breaks.

       1   2   3   4   5

Extremely   Extremely

Uncharacteristic of Me   *Characteristic* of Me

17. Some of my friends think I'm a hothead.

       1   2   3   4   5

Extremely   Extremely

Uncharacteristic of Me   *Characteristic* of Me

18. I can't help getting into arguments when people disagree with me.

       1   2   3   4   5

Extremely   Extremely

Uncharacteristic of Me   *Characteristic* of Me

19. I can think of no good reason for ever hitting a person.

       1   2   3   4   5

Extremely   Extremely

Uncharacteristic of Me   *Characteristic* of Me

20. I have trouble controlling my temper.

       1   2   3   4   5

Extremely   Extremely

Uncharacteristic of Me   *Characteristic* of Me

21. I sometimes feel that people are laughing at me behind my back.

       1   2   3   4   5

Extremely   Extremely

Uncharacteristic of Me   *Characteristic* of Me

22. If somebody hits me, I hit back.

       1   2   3   4   5

Extremely   Extremely

Uncharacteristic of Me   *Characteristic* of Me

23. I often find myself disagreeing with people.

1	2	3	4	5

Extremely
Uncharacteristic of Me

Extremely
Characteristic of Me

24. I have threatened people I know.

1	2	3	4	5

Extremely
Uncharacteristic of Me

Extremely
Characteristic of Me

25. When frustrated, I let my irritation show.

1	2	3	4	5

Extremely
Uncharacteristic of Me

Extremely
Characteristic of Me

26. I know that "friends" talk about me behind my back.

1	2	3	4	5

Extremely
Uncharacteristic of Me

Extremely
Characteristic of Me

27. I am an even-tempered person.

1	2	3	4	5

Extremely
Uncharacteristic of Me

Extremely
Characteristic of Me

28. I get into fights a little more than the average person.

1	2	3	4	5

Extremely
Uncharacteristic of Me

Extremely
Characteristic of Me

29. At times I feel I have gotten a raw deal out of life.

1	2	3	4	5

Extremely
Uncharacteristic of Me

Extremely
Characteristic of Me

Scoring

The Aggression Questionnaire, developed by Arnold Buss and Mark Perry (1992), consists of four subscales: Physical Aggression, Verbal Aggression, Anger, and Hostility.

Physical Aggression - add scores on items 1, 5, 9, 13, 14, 19, 22, 24, and 28 after reversing scores (1 = 5, 2 = 4, 3 = 3, 4 = 2 and 5 = 1) on item 19. Score _____

Verbal Aggression - add scores on items 2, 6, 12, 18 and 23. Score _____

Anger - add scores on items 4, 8, 11, 17, 20, 25, and 27 after reversing your score on item 27. Score _____

Hostility - add scores on items 3, 7, 10, 15, 16, 21, 26, and 29. Score _____

Total Score - add scores of all four scales   Score _____

The authors reported the following means and standard deviations for men and women. On the Physical Aggression scale, men had a mean of 24.3 (SD = 7.7) and women had a mean of 17.9 (SD = 6.6). On the Verbal Aggression scale, men had a mean of 15.2 (SD = 3.9) and women had a mean of 13.5 (SD = 3.9). On the Anger Scale, men had a mean of 17.0 (SD = 5.6) and women had a mean of 16.7 (SD = 5.8). On the Hostility scale, men had a mean of 21.3 (SD = 5.5) and women had a mean of 20.2 (SD = 6.3). For Total scores, men had a mean of 77.8 (SD = 16.5) and women had a mean of 68.2 (SD = 17.0).

How well do your scores on these subscales relate to your experience? Explain.

Reference

Buss, A. H., & Perry, M. (1992). The aggression questionnaire. *Journal of Personality and Social Psychology, 63*, 452-459.

Name _____

Active Learning Experience

8.2 Adaptation and Deprivation

1. Imagine that, upon graduation, you get a job in your field of interest. How much would you expect your yearly salary to be?

   $ _____

   On a 10-point scale, rate your level of satisfaction with that salary.

1	2	3	4	5	6	7	8	9	10
low									high

   Now, imagine that you find out that the salary you indicated above is 20% *lower* than the average salary of your classmates who got jobs in your field.

   How satisfied would you be with your salary then?

1	2	3	4	5	6	7	8	9	10
low									high

2. What would you consider a "good" yearly income for a single person to live on?

   $ _____

How would you describe your family's income over the past 5 years (or, if you have been independent of your family, describe your income over the past 5 years).

   low   _____

   low to average _____

   average   _____

   average to high _____

   high   _____

These two activities are designed to assess the role of relative comparisons in determining life satisfaction or frustration. In the first activity, if you rated your satisfaction lower than your original rating after comparing it to your classmates' salaries, you are experiencing relative deprivation (perceiving yourself as less well off than your classmates). Frustration is a likely reaction to relative deprivation.

The second task involves adaptation level--the tendency to adapt to a level of stimulation and to react to changes from that level. In this case, most people determine a good yearly income based on the level they are accustomed to. As you examine the income levels set by yourself and others, you should note discrepancies based on how high or low their previous income was. Again, frustration can arise when individuals experience a negative deviation from their previously experienced income level.

Can you demonstrate the roles of relative deprivation and adaptation level in other areas of your life?

Relative deprivation -

Adaptation level -

Name _____

Active Learning Experience

8.3 Sex Attitudes

Before reading further, indicate the extent of your agreement or disagreement with the following questions on the 7 point scale.

1. A woman who goes to the home or apartment of a man on their first date implies that she is willing to have sex.

1	2	3	4	5	6	7
Strongly Disagree						Strongly Agree

2. Any female can get raped.

1	2	3	4	5	6	7
Strongly Disagree						Strongly Agree

3. One reason that women falsely report a rape is that they frequently have a need to call attention to themselves.

1	2	3	4	5	6	7
Strongly Disagree						Strongly Agree

4. Any healthy woman can successfully resist a rapist if she really wants to.

1	2	3	4	5	6	7
Strongly Disagree						Strongly Agree

5. When women go around braless or wearing short skirts and tight tops, they are just asking for trouble.

1	2	3	4	5	6	7
Strongly Disagree						Strongly Agree

6. In the majority of rapes, the victim is promiscuous or has a bad reputation.

    1   2   3   4   5   6   7
    Strongly   Strongly
    Disagree   Agree

7. If a girl engages in necking or petting and she lets things get out of hand, it is her own fault if her partner forces sex on her.

    1   2   3   4   5   6   7
    Strongly   Strongly
    Disagree   Agree

8. Women who get raped while hitchhiking get what they deserve.

    1   2   3   4   5   6   7
    Strongly   Strongly
    Disagree   Agree

9. A woman who is stuck-up and thinks she is too good to talk to guys on the street deserves to be taught a lesson.

    1   2   3   4   5   6   7
    Strongly   Strongly
    Disagree   Agree

10. Many women have an unconscious wish to be raped, and may then unconsciously set up a situation in which they are likely to be attacked.

    1   2   3   4   5   6   7
    Strongly   Strongly
    Disagree   Agree

11. If a woman gets drunk at a party and has intercourse with a man she's just met there, she should be considered "fair game" to other males at the party who want to have sex with her too, whether she wants to or not.

    1   2   3   4   5   6   7
    Strongly   Strongly
    Disagree   Agree

From Burt, M. R. (1980). Cultural myths and supports for rape. *Journal of Personality and Social Psychology, 38*, 217-230. Copyright © 1980 by the American Psychological Association. Reprinted with permission.

Interpretation

All of the items are false, except number 2.

The scale (which is reproduced only in part) that these items were drawn from was developed by Martha Burt (1980) to help us understand and change the rape "myth--defined as prejudicial, stereotyped, or false beliefs about rape, rape victims, and rapists" (p. 217).

Burt noted in her discussion that many Americans believe many of these rape myths, and that their beliefs are strongly related to sex role stereotyping, distrust of the opposite sex, and even acceptance of interpersonal violence. With respect to the scale, she found that over half of her subjects agreed with questions 1 and 6.

What is your reaction to the scale and your individual responses?

134

Would you expect gender differences on this scale? Explain.

References

Burt, M. R. (1980). Cultural myths and supports for rape. *Journal of Personality and Social Psychology, 38,* 217-230.

CHAPTER 9

Altruism

Name _____

Active Learning Experience

9.1 Volunteerism

Read the following scenarios and respond to the questions following each.

Imagine that your community's Volunteer Emergency Service is recruiting to fill positions in three areas. Read each of the positions and respond to the questions following each one.

Position 1. Volunteer to work with emergency medical technicians and paramedics in on-scene assessment, treatment, and transport of patients to the hospital.

Indicate the degree to which you would like to participate in this activity.

1	2	3	4	5
would *not* like to participate at all				would *very* much like to participate

Indicate the degree to which you would anticipate experiencing each of these reactions in this volunteer position.

sympathy

1	2	3	4	5
would not feel this way at all				would feel this way very much

compassion

1	2	3	4	5
would not feel this way at all				would feel this way very much

distress

1	2	3	4	5
would not feel this way at all				would feel this way very much

anxiety

1	2	3	4	5
would not feel this way at all				would feel this way very much

enjoyment

1	2	3	4	5
would not feel this way at all				would feel this way very much

satisfaction

1	2	3	4	5
would not feel this way at all				would feel this way very much

Position 2. Volunteer to work with patients and their families in an after-care program providing emotional and practical support to aid recovery.

Indicate the degree to which you would like to participate in this activity.

1	2	3	4	5
would *not* like to participate at all				would *very* much like to participate

Indicate the degree to which you would anticipate experiencing each of these reactions in this volunteer position.

sympathy

1	2	3	4	5
would not feel this way at all				would feel this way very much

compassion

1	2	3	4	5
would not feel this way at all				would feel this way very much

distress

1	2	3	4	5
would not feel this way at all				would feel this way very much

anxiety

1	2	3	4	5
would not feel this way at all				would feel this way very much

enjoyment

1	2	3	4	5
would not feel this way at all				would feel this way very much

satisfaction

1	2	3	4	5
would not feel this way at all				would feel this way very much

Position 3. Volunteer to work on community awareness and fundraising--developing informational brochures and fundraising letters, contacting potential organizational and individual donors.

Indicate the degree to which you would like to participate in this activity.

1	2	3	4	5
would *not* like to participate at all				would *very* much like to participate

Indicate the degree to which you would anticipate experiencing each of these reactions in this volunteer position.

sympathy

1	2	3	4	5
would not feel this way at all				would feel this way very much

compassion

1	2	3	4	5
would not feel this way at all				would feel this way very much

distress

1	2	3	4	5
would not feel this way at all				would feel this way very much

anxiety

1	2	3	4	5
would not feel this way at all				would feel this way very much

enjoyment

1	2	3	4	5
would not feel this way at all				would feel this way very much

satisfaction

1	2	3	4	5
would not feel this way at all				would feel this way very much

Rank the three positions in terms of your interest in volunteering in them.

1.   2.   3.

This activity was adapted from the research of Mark Davis and his colleagues (1999) on the process by which volunteers come to work in particular settings. They found that greater situational feelings of sympathy and lesser feelings of distress contributed to satisfaction.

How did your ratings on these factors correspond to your decision making? [Calculate your averages for the three variables by averaging the scores on the two items for each: sympathy (sympathy + compassion), distress (distress and anxiety), and satisfaction (enjoyment and satisfaction)]. Explain.

1. On-scene volunteer
   Sympathy average _____
   Distress average _____
   Satisfaction average _____

2. After-care volunteer
   Sympathy average _____
   Distress average _____
   Satisfaction average _____

3. Fund raising volunteers
   Sympathy average   _____
   Distress average   _____
   Satisfaction average _____

Reference

Davis, M. H., Mitchell, K. V., Hall, J. A., Lothert, J., Snapp, T., & Meyer, M. (1999). Empathy, expectations, and situational preferences: Personality influences on the decision to participate in volunteer helping behavior. *Journal of Personality, 67,* 469-503.

Name _____

Active Learning Experience

9.2 Interpersonal Reactivity Index

Mark Davis (1980) was also interested in assessing interpersonal reactivity. **Before reading further**, complete the following questionnaire.

Respond to each of the items by circling the appropriate number.

1. When I am reading an interesting story or novel, I imagine how I would feel if the events in the story were happening to me.

0	1	2	3	4
does not describe me well			describes me very well	

2. I really get involved with the feelings of the characters in a novel.

0	1	2	3	4
does not describe me well			describes me very well	

3. I am usually objective when I watch a movie or play, and I don't often get completely caught up in it.

0	1	2	3	4
does not describe me well			describes me very well	

4. After seeing a play or movie, I have felt as though I were one of the characters.

0	1	2	3	4
does not describe me well			describes me very well	

5. I daydream and fantasize, with some regularity, about things that might happen to me.

0	1	2	3	4
does not describe me well			describes me very well	

6. Becoming extremely involved in a good book or movie is somewhat rare for me.

0	1	2	3	4
does not describe me well			describes me very well	

7. When I watch a good movie, I can very easily put myself in the place of a leading character.

0	1	2	3	4
does not describe me well			describes me very well	

8. Before criticizing somebody, I try to imagine how I would feel if I were in their place.

0	1	2	3	4
does not describe me well			describes me very well	

9. If I'm sure I'm right about something, I don't waste much time listening to other people's arguments.

0	1	2	3	4
does not describe me well			describes me very well	

10. I sometimes try to understand my friends better by imagining how things look from their perspective.

                0   1   2   3   4
        does not describe me well   describes me very well

11. I believe that there are two sides to every question and try to look at them both.

                0   1   2   3   4
        does not describe me well   describes me very well

12. I sometimes find it difficult to see things from the "other guy's" point of view.

                0   1   2   3   4
        does not describe me well   describes me very well

13. I try to look at everybody's side of a disagreement before I make a decision.

                0   1   2   3   4
        does not describe me well   describes me very well

14. When I'm upset at someone, I usually try to "put myself in his shoes" for a while.

                0   1   2   3   4
        does not describe me well   describes me very well

15. When I see someone being taken advantage of, I feel kind of protective towards them.

                0   1   2   3   4
        does not describe me well   describes me very well

16. When I see someone being treated unfairly, I sometimes don't feel very much pity for them.

                0   1   2   3   4
        does not describe me well   describes me very well

17. I often have tender, concerned feelings for people less fortunate than me.

                0   1   2   3   4
        does not describe me well   describes me very well

18. I would describe myself as a pretty soft-hearted person.

                0   1   2   3   4
        does not describe me well   describes me very well

19. Sometimes I don't feel very sorry for other people when they are having problems.

                0   1   2   3   4
        does not describe me well   describes me very well

20. Other people's misfortunes do not usually disturb me a great deal.

                0   1   2   3   4
        does not describe me well   describes me very well

21. I am often quite touched by things that I see happen.

                0   1   2   3   4
        does not describe me well   describes me very well

22. When I see someone who badly needs help in an emergency, I go to pieces.

     0   1   2   3   4

does not describe me well   describes me very well

23. I sometimes feel helpless when I am in the middle of a very emotional situation.

     0   1   2   3   4

does not describe me well   describes me very well

24. In emergency situations, I feel apprehensive and ill-at-ease.

     0   1   2   3   4

does not describe me well   describes me very well

25. I am usually pretty effective in dealing with emergencies.

     0   1   2   3   4

does not describe me well   describes me very well

26. Being in a tense emotional situation scares me.

     0   1   2   3   4

does not describe me well   describes me very well

27. When I see someone hurt, I tend to remain calm.

     0   1   2   3   4

does not describe me well   describes me very well

28. I tend to lose control during emergencies.

     0   1   2   3   4

does not describe me well   describes me very well

Scoring: There are four subscales, each composed of seven items. On scale 1, "Fantasy," (items 1-7), questions 1, 2, 3, 5, and 7 are scored directly and question 3 and 6 are reversed (i.e., change 0 to 4, 1 to 3, 3 to 1, and 4 to 0). Add the total of the seven questions.

Total "fantasy" score _____

On section 2, "Perspective-taking," (items 8-14), questions 8, 10, 11, 13, and 14 are scored directly and questions 9 and 12 reversed. Add the total of the seven questions.

Total "perspective-taking" score _____

On scale 3, "empathic concern," (items 15-21), questions 15, 17, 18, and 21 are scored directly and questions 16, 19, and 20 are reversed. Add the total of the seven questions.

Total "empathic concern" score _____

On scale 4, "Personal distress," (items 22-28), questions 22, 23, 24, 26, and 28 are scored directly and questions 25 and 27 are reversed. Add the total of the seven questions.

Total "personal distress" score _____

Davis (1980) reported the following means for college undergraduates:

Scale	Men	Women
Fantasy	15.73	18.75
Perspective-taking	16.78	17.96
Empathic concern	19.04	21.67
Personal distresses	12.18	9.46

How do your scores relate to your actual "helping" attitudes and behaviors?

How would you explain gender differences on this scale?

Davis and his colleagues (1999) wrote that dispositional empathy not only affects individuals' helping behavior when needed, but their willingness to encounter needy people in the first place. For example, Davis (1983) found that individuals high in dispositional empathic concern not only reported giving more to the muscular dystrophy telethon, they were more likely to be watching the telethon!

So, scores on this index may indicate more than your willingness to help when the need arises. They may tell you how well suited you are for a career in a helping profession.

Do the results of this activity influence your thoughts about possible career choices? Explain.

References

Davis, M. H. (1980). A multidimensional approach to individual differences in empathy. *JSAS Catalog of Selected Documents in Psychology, 10,* 85.

Davis, M. H. (1983). Empathic concerns and the muscular dystrophy telethon: Empathy as a multidimensional construct. *Personality and Social Psychology Bulletin, 9,* 223-229.

Davis, M. H., Mitchell, K. V., Hall, J. A., Lothert, J., Snapp, T., & Meyer, M. (1999). Empathy, expectations, and situational preferences: Personality influences on the decision to participate in volunteer helping behaviors. *Journal of Personality, 67,* 469-503.

Name _____

Active Learning Experience

9.3 Reciprocity

The following two activities will help you understand the reciprocity norm.

1. Throughout the course of a day or two, randomly select 20 people and briefly make eye contact with them. For half of these encounters, smile and say "hi"! For the other half, make brief eye contact but do ***not*** smile or say anything.

    Keep a record of the number of people in the two groups that smile and/or respond verbally. You may need to enlist the help of a classmate to walk behind you and record people's reactions.

	# of Responses Smile	Verbalization	Both
Smile--hi group			
Non smile--hi group			

2. List the names of the non family members that currently give you gifts or have given gifts to you in the past for special occasions (e.g., birthdays, holidays, etc.).

Put a check mark next to those who you also give (gave) gifts to on these occasions.

These are examples of the reciprocity norm. We expect others to treat us positively after we have treated them positively. Evolutionary psychologists believe that this principle increased cooperation among individuals and helped ensure survival of those who adopted it.

Can you describe some other situations where this norm has influenced people's behavior?

CHAPTER 10

Interpersonal Attraction and Relationships

Name _____

Active Learning Experience

10.1 Dating and Mating

Before reading further, follow the directions below.

This activity, based on the research of Bill Tooke and Lori Camire (1991), will investigate particular actions and strategies that people employ as a means to appear more desirable to members of the opposite sex than they really are.

List the "best five strategies that you or others of your sex can employ to make yourself more desirable to members of the opposite sex than you really are.

1.

2.

3.

4.

5.

Now, list the best five strategies that members of the opposite sex could employ to make themselves appear more desirable to members of your sex than they really are.

1.

2.

3.

4.

5.

If you were to place an ad in the "Personals" section of the newspaper, how would you describe *yourself* and how would you describe the kind of person you are *seeking*?

Your description:

Description of person you are seeking:

In comparing the two parts of each activity, are there similarities? Differences?

Explain.

156

Research generally demonstrates differences in how men and women approach dating and mating situations. For example, Tooke and Camire (1991) found significant sex differences in deceptive behaviors. Males reported using more tactics referring to dominance and resources (e.g., spending money, acting dominant, wearing expensive clothes, embellishing career expectations), and exaggerated sincerity, trust, and kindness. Females reported using more tactics involving enhancement of bodily appearance. Similar results have been reported (Buss, 1994) for personal ads. Women are looking for men who are older, more stable and secure, and good financial prospects. They emphasize physical attractiveness and youth in themselves. Men highlight their prospects for financial security and look for women who are younger and physically attractive.

How well do these findings reflect your experiences?

References

Buss, D. (1994). The strategies of human mating. *American Scientist, 82*, 238-250.
Tooke, W., & Camire, L. (1991). Patterned deceptions in intersexual and intrasexual mating strategies. *Ethology & Sociobiology, 12,* 345-364.

Name _____

Active Learning Experience

10.2 Passionate Love

THE PASSIONATE LOVE SCALE

Think of the person you love most passionately *right now*. (If you are not in love right now, think of the last person you loved passionately. If you have never been in love, think of the person whom you came closest to caring for in that way.) Describe how you felt at the time when your feelings were the most intense.

Possible answers range from:

(1)	(2)	(3)	(4)	(5)	(6)	(7)	(8)	(9)
Not at all True				Moderately True				Definitely True

1.   I would feel deep despair if _____ left me.

         1   2   3   4   5   6   7   8   9

2.   Sometimes I feel I can't control my thoughts: they are obsessively on _____.

         1   2   3   4   5   6   7   8   9

3.   I feel happy when I am doing something to make _____ happy.

         1   2   3   4   5   6   7   8   9

4.   I would rather be with _____ than anyone else.

         1   2   3   4   5   6   7   8   9

5.   I'd get jealous if I thought _____ were falling in love with someone else.

         1   2   3   4   5   6   7   8   9

6. I yearn to know all about _____.

    1   2   3   4   5   6   7   8   9

7. I want _____ --physically, emotionally, mentally.

    1   2   3   4   5   6   7   8   9

8. I have an endless appetite for affection from _____.

    1   2   3   4   5   6   7   8   9

9. For me, _____ is the perfect romantic partner.

    1   2   3   4   5   6   7   8   9

10. I sense my body responding when _____ touches me.

    1   2   3   4   5   6   7   8   9

11. _____ always seems to be on my mind.

    1   2   3   4   5   6   7   8   9

12. I want _____ to know me--my thoughts, my fears, and my hopes.

    1   2   3   4   5   6   7   8   9

13. I eagerly look for signs indicating _____'s desire for me.

    1   2   3   4   5   6   7   8   9

14. I possess a powerful attraction for _____.

    1   2   3   4   5   6   7   8   9

15. I get extremely depressed when things don't go right in my relationship
    with _____.

    1   2   3   4   5   6   7   8   9

Scoring: Total your score for the 15 items:

Score _____

The following table will show you how your score compares to those of other college students.

Score	Percentile
129	99
122	95
118	90
113	80
110	70
107	60
102	50
98	40
85	30
74	20
68	10
65	5
51	1

The higher your score, the more intense the passion you feel in the relationship.

Interpersonal attraction is a popular topic in social psychology. And no discussion of interpersonal attraction would be complete without touching on the subject of love. As Elaine Hatfield and Richard Rapson (1996) noted "passionate love is seen as a magic elixir for finding fulfillment in life, as heady a brew as power, money, freedom" (p. 155). The *Passionate Love Scale* was designed by Elaine Hatfield and Susan Sprecher (1986) to assess the intense longing for union with another. This is a version of the scale (Hatfield and Rapson, 1993).

Passionate love has its obvious delights, and research has shown that it can even be good for your immune system! But, as Hatfield and Rapson (1996) show, it can have a dark side too. "Passionate lovers may panic when confronted with the prospect of dealing with someone they have idealized. They may suffer [feel emptiness, anxiety, or despair] when they find their love is unrequited. They may discover they are extremely jealous. They may feel mortified, miserable, stung, and bruised. They may squabble; squabbles may escalate into sharp words and even violence." (p. 166). Some of these dimensions are assessed in the questionnaire.

Hatfield (1995) also noted that we need to be vigilant. We are most vulnerable to passionate love relationships (which are most likely doomed to failure) when our self-esteem has been shaken, or when we feel dependent, insecure, anxious, fearful, or needy. Forewarned is forearmed!

How does passionate love affect various aspects of your life?

Personal:

Social:

Academic:

In examining your total score as well as your responses to particular items, are there areas that you would like to change? If so, why? How can you accomplish this change?

162

References

Hatfield, E. (1995). Self-esteem and passionate love relationships. In G. G. Brannigan and M. R. Merrens (Eds.), *The social psychologists: Research adventures.* New York: McGraw-Hill.

Hatfield, E., & Rapson, R. L. (1993). *Love, sex, and intimacy: Their psychology, biology, and history.* New York: HarperCollins.

Hatfield, E., & Rapson, R. L. (1996). *Love & sex: Cross-cultural perspectives.* Boston: Allyn & Bacon.

Hatfield, E., & Sprecher, S. (1986). Measuring passionate love in intimate relations. *Journal of Adolescence, 9*, 383-410.

Scale from Hatfield, E., & Rapson, R. L. (1993). *Love, sex, and intimacy: Their psychology, biology, and history.* New York: HarperCollins. Reprinted with permission.

Name _____

Active Learning Experience

10.3 Relationships

David Myers (1999) summarized research on marriage and divorce, and identified several factors that contribute to marital success. I have asked students in my classes to examine these factors for their parents' marriage, and consistently found significant differences between those parents still married in comparison to those separated/divorced.

Identify which factors characterize your parents' marriage.

Married after age 20 _____

Both grew up in stable, two-parent homes _____

Dated for at least 1 year before marriage _____

Are well (at least high school graduates) and similarly educated _____

Enjoy a good, stable income _____

Live in a small town or on a farm _____

Did not cohabit or become pregnant before marriage _____

Are within three years of one another in age _____

Are of similar faith and religiously committed _____

Are your parents still married? _____

Are your parents separated/divorced? _____

Number of similarities and maturity factors listed _____

Your instructor can compare the scores for those still married versus those separated/divorced. What was the result for your class?

164

This activity focuses on the roles of maturity and similarity in relationship longevity. Unfortunately, as Baron and Byrne (1997) noted "we can easily 'overlook' or discount areas of dissimilarity because of attributes such as physical attractiveness, the possession of material resources, and so forth. So we make compromises... As a result, the negative attributes (such as dissimilar attitudes) that didn't seem all that important at first can later have a negative effect on marital success (p. 303).

You may want to consider these factors in your previous, current, and future relationships!

References

Baron, R. A., & Byrne, D. (1997). *Social psychology* (8th ed.). Boston: Allyn & Bacon.

Myers, D. G. (1999). *Social psychology* (6th Ed). New York: McGraw-Hill.

CHAPTER 11

Applied Social Psychology

Name _____

Active Learning Experience

11.1 Attributions

Imagine that you received a letter from your bank stating that an error has been found in your checking account. Think about the possible reasons why this error may have occurred. What would be the *most* likely reason for the error?

Answer the following three questions.

1. Does the reason you cited reflect something about you (Internal) or something about other people or outside circumstances (External)?

2. Does the reason reflect something permanent (Stable) or something temporary (Unstable)?

3. Does the reason reflect something that affects a variety of situations (Global), or is it unique to this situation (Specific).

There are eight combinations of these three dimensions. Circle the one that fits your reason for the error.

1	Internal-Stable-Specific
2	Internal-Stable-Global
3	Internal-Unstable-Specific
4	Internal-Unstable-Global
5	External-Stable-Specific
6	External-Stable-Global
7	External-Unstable-Specific
8	External-Unstable-Global

Christopher Peterson and Martin Seligman (1984) noted that our attributions have important implications for our psychological well-being. The *locus* of attributions (Internal or External) affects self-esteem. An internal attribution for a negative event may lower self-esteem, while an external attribution is less likely to affect self-esteem. The *stability* of attributions affects the duration of our emotional reaction. A stable attribution for a negative event is likely to result in persistent feelings of anger or depression, while an unstable attribution would have a less persistent effect. The extent of attributions (Global or Specific) affects the pervasiveness of situations encompassed by the reaction. A global attribution extends to a wide variety of situations. A specific attribution is focused on a particular situation. For example, if one attributes success to "being good at everything" (Internal-Stable-Global), it will likely lead to increased self-esteem, a sense of pride, and expectations for success in many situations. If one attributes failure to "life is unfair" (External-Stable-Global), it may lead to an expectation for failure in the future, a sense of powerlessness, and anger. Internal, stable, global attributions for failure, as Peterson and Seligman noted, may lead to the development of depression and learned helplessness.

As you analyze your own attributions, you will get a clearer picture of how behavior influences thoughts, which further influence behavior. One reason for studying psychology is to gain this insight. A second is to realize that change is possible and that we are capable of bringing about this change ourselves.

Are these attributions typical of how you view your successes and failures? Explain.

What role do your attributions play in your life?

Are there specific areas of your life where there are clearly recognizable patterns? Explain.

How have gender and cultural factors affected your attributions?

How can you go about changing attributional patterns or tendencies?

Reference

Peterson, C., & Seligman, M. (1984). Causal explanations as a risk factor for depression: Theory and evidence, *Psychological Review, 91,* 347-374.

Name _____

Active Learning Experience

11.2 Legal Opinions

Before reading further, answer the questions on the legal opinions survey below.

Legal Opinions Survey

This is a questionnaire designed by Saul Kassin and Lawrence Wrightsman (1983) to determine legal attitudes and beliefs. Answer each statement by giving as true a picture of your own beliefs as possible.

1. Appointed judges are more competent than elected judges.

A	B	C	D	E
Strongly Agree	Mildly Agree	Undecided	Mostly Disagree	Strongly Disagree

2. A defendant should be found guilty if 11 out of 12 jurors vote guilty.

A	B	C	D	E
Strongly Agree	Mildly Agree	Undecided	Mostly Disagree	Strongly Disagree

3. Too often jurors hesitate to convict someone who is guilty out of pure sympathy.

A	B	C	D	E
Strongly Agree	Mildly Agree	Undecided	Mostly Disagree	Strongly Disagree

4. In most cases where the accused presents a strong defense, it is only because of a good lawyer.

A	B	C	D	E
Strongly Agree	Mildly Agree	Undecided	Mostly Disagree	Strongly Disagree

5. The death penalty is cruel and inhumane.

A	B	C	D	E
Strongly Agree	Mildly Agree	Undecided	Mostly Disagree	Strongly Disagree

6. Out of every 100 people brought to trial, at least 75 are guilty of the crime with which they are charged.

A	B	C	D	E
Strongly Agree	Mildly Agree	Undecided	Mostly Disagree	Strongly Disagree

7. For serious crimes like murder, a defendant should be found guilty so long as there is a 90% chance that he committed the crime.

A	B	C	D	E
Strongly Agree	Mildly Agree	Undecided	Mostly Disagree	Strongly Disagree

8. Defense lawyers don't really care about guilt or innocence, they are just in business to make money.

A	B	C	D	E
Strongly Agree	Mildly Agree	Undecided	Mostly Disagree	Strongly Disagree

9. Generally, the police make an arrest only when they are sure about who committed the crime.

A	B	C	D	E
Strongly Agree	Mildly Agree	Undecided	Mostly Disagree	Strongly Disagree

10. Circumstantial evidence is too weak to use in court.

A	B	C	D	E
Strongly Agree	Mildly Agree	Undecided	Mostly Disagree	Strongly Disagree

11. Many accident claims filed against insurance companies are phony.

A	B	C	D	E
Strongly Agree	Mildly Agree	Undecided	Mostly Disagree	Strongly Disagree

12. The defendant is often a victim of his own bad reputation.

A	B	C	D	E
Strongly Agree	Mildly Agree	Undecided	Mostly Disagree	Strongly Disagree

13. If the grand jury recommends that a person be brought to trial, then he probably committed the crime.

A	B	C	D	E
Strongly Agree	Mildly Agree	Undecided	Mostly Disagree	Strongly Disagree

14. Extenuating circumstances should not be considered--if a person commits a crime, then that person should be punished.

A	B	C	D	E
Strongly Agree	Mildly Agree	Undecided	Mostly Disagree	Strongly Disagree

15. Too many innocent people are wrongfully imprisoned.

A	B	C	D	E
Strongly Agree	Mildly Agree	Undecided	Mostly Disagree	Strongly Disagree

16. If a majority of the evidence--but not all of it--suggests that the defendant committed the crime, the jury should vote *not guilty*.

A	B	C	D	E
Strongly Agree	Mildly Agree	Undecided	Mostly Disagree	Strongly Disagree

17. If the defendant committed a victimless crime like gambling or possession of marijuana, he should never be convicted.

A	B	C	D	E
Strongly Agree	Mildly Agree	Undecided	Mostly Disagree	Strongly Disagree

From Kassin, S. M., & Wrightsman, L. S. (1983). The construction and validation of a juror bias scale. *Journal of Research in Personality, 17,* 423-442. Copyright © 1983 by Academic Press. Reprinted with permission.

Scoring

For questions 1, 2, 3, 4, 6, 7, 8, 9, 11, 13, and 14
    A = 5, B = 4, C = 3, D = 2, and E = 1.
For questions 5, 10, 12, 15, 16, and 17
    A = 1, B = 2, C = 3, D = 4, and E = 5.

Total your scores _____

Kassin and Wrightsman (1983) reported a range of scores from 39 to 66. The mean for their sample was 50.88, and the standard deviation was 7.01.

The scale was intended to measure pretrial bias in jurors. Specifically, the scale assesses jurors' generalized expectancies that defendants commit the crimes they are charged with. It also assesses the value they associated with conviction and punishment of criminals. As a result, those scoring higher on the scale would be considered pro-prosecution, and those scoring lower on the scale would be considered pro-defense.

How does your score compare to their mean? _____

If your score was biased in one direction or the other, how do you account for it?

How could you keep this bias in check if you were to serve on a jury?

Reference

Kassin, S. M., & Wrightsman, L. S. (1983). The construction and validation of a juror bias scale. *Journal of Research in Personality, 17,* 423-442.

Name _____

Active Learning Experience

11.3 Decision Making

Imagine the following situation.

You are a member of the Planning Board in the town in which you grew up. The economic picture for the town has been bleak for several years, and many people you have known all your life are without jobs. A large company submitted a plan to the Board to build a manufacturing plant that will bring needed jobs to the town and raise the standard of living. However, the manufacturing process will produce emissions that will cause irreparable damage to forest land, rivers, and lakes in the area.

How would you weigh each of the following factors in your decision making process for or against the proposed company?

1. The Environment -
       1   2   3   4   5
    No Importance   Great Importance

2. Economics -
       1   2   3   4   5
    No Importance   Great Importance

3. Relationships with other townspeople -
       1   2   3   4   5
    No Importance   Great Importance

What was the single most important factor for you?

How would you vote?

For the company _____

Against the company _____

This story was loosely based on the research of Lawrence Axelrod (1994), who found that personal values have a dramatic effect on people's decision making. He compared three types of value orientation: Universally orientated--making decisions for the betterment of the world, even if they involve social and/or economic costs; Socially oriented--making decisions based on concerns for relationships with others; and Economically oriented--making decisions based on material gain. People's general value orientations did affect their decisions in situations like the one posed here. Specifically, Universally-oriented people were more likely to make environmentally protective decisions, economically-oriented people were more likely to make economically advantageous decisions, and socially-oriented people were more likely to make decisions based on how they would affect relationships with others.

Do you feel that you fit more clearly into one of these value orientations than the others? Explain.

How does your value orientation affect other decisions in your day-to-day life, especially those that involve conflict with other values?

Reference

Axelrod, L. J. (1994). Balancing personal needs with environmental preservation: Identifying the values that guide decisions in ecological dilemmas. *Journal of Social Issues, 50,* 85-104.